True Love

Coupons

SOURCEBOOKS, INC.
NAPERVILLE, ILLINOIS

Published by Sourcebooks, Inc., P.O. Box 4410, Naperville, IL 60567-4410
630.961.3900 Fax: 630.961.2168

Printed and bound in the United States of America
HS 10 9 8 7 6 5 4 3 2

True Love Coupons

This coupon is redeemable for a full body massage, complete with relaxing music, scented oils, and warm hands

special notes:

This coupon is good for one delicious breakfast in bed

special notes:

This coupon is redeemable for a trip to a lingerie boutique, where the coupon-giver will purchase any item of the coupon-holder's choice

special notes:

_____

_____

_____

_____

_____

_____

Because I love you,
I will take you
out to a romantic
restaurant for dinner

special notes:

_____

_____

_____

_____

_____

This coupon
is good for
101 passionate
kisses

special notes:

_____

_____

_____

_____

_____

_____

This coupon entitles you to a romantic weekend getaway of your choice

special notes:

_____

_____

_____

_____

_____

_____

This coupon entitles you to hundreds of sweet nothings and sexy suggestions to be whispered in your ear

special notes:
_____
_____
_____
_____
_____
_____

True Love Coupons

This coupon is good for an adventurous weekend getaway of your choice

special notes:

Because you mean so much, I will make you a delicious, candlelight dinner at home

special notes:

True Love Coupons

This coupon is redeemable for a romantic, stress-free lunch break at your favorite restaurant

special notes:

True Love Coupons

To celebrate fall, let's take a walk in the woods and visit local pumpkin patches and apple orchards

special notes:

_____

_____

_____

_____

_____

_____

True Love Coupons

This coupon entitles you to a picnic in a park, all supplies provided by the coupon-giver

special notes:

_____

_____

_____

_____

_____

_____

This coupon is redeemable for lots of cuddling in front of a warm fireplace

special notes:
_____
_____
_____
_____
_____
_____

Because I love you,
I will take you on
a horse-drawn carriage
ride through your
favorite city—lots of
snuggling included

special notes:

This coupon is good for an evening of cuddling on the couch in front of your favorite romantic movie

special notes:

This coupon is redeemable for a dozen long-stemmed red roses

special notes:

_____

_____

_____

_____

_____

_____

True Love Coupons

This coupon
is good for one
full day of
pampering—
no requests
will be denied!

special notes:

_____

_____

_____

_____

_____

_____

This coupon entitles you to a house filled with flowers!

special notes:

True Love Coupons

Because I love you, I will bring home a bottle of your favorite wine

Special notes:

_____

_____

_____

_____

_____

_____

This coupon is good for a romantic stroll along your favorite country path

special notes:

True Love

Coupons

This coupon is redeemable for a foot massage lasting at least twenty minutes

special notes:
_____
_____
_____
_____
_____
_____

This coupon entitles you to a weekend in your favorite local hotel, with Jacuzzis, room service, and endless TV-free time included

special notes:

_____

_____

_____

_____

_____

_____

Because you're so sweet, I will bring you a box of your favorite chocolates

special notes:

This coupon is good for an adventurous weekend getaway of your choice

special notes:

True
Love
Coupons

This coupon
entitles you to
a phone call for no
other purpose than
to tell you how
much I love you

special notes:

True Love Coupons

This coupon entitles you to hundreds of sweet nothings and sexy suggestions to be whispered in your ear

special notes:

This coupon is good for a delicious and romantic Sunday brunch to be prepared and served by the coupon-giver

special notes:

True Love Coupons

Because you are my true love, I will take you out for a romantic evening on the town, and cost is no object

special notes:

True Love Coupons

To celebrate winter, let's build a snowman and make snow angels together, then cuddle in front of a warm fire with hot chocolate

special notes:

This coupon entitles you to an evening of dinner and dancing

Special notes:

This coupon is good for the dessert of your choice, baked by the coupon-giver

special notes:

This coupon is redeemable for a weekend at the beach

Special notes:

_____

_____

_____

_____

_____

_____

True Love Coupons

This coupon is good for a skiing trip, lots of hot chocolate and cuddling in the lodge included

special notes:

True Love Coupons

Because I love you, I will bring you a bouquet of your favorite flowers

special notes:

To celebrate spring, let's go fly a kite!

Special notes:

_____

_____

_____

_____

_____

_____

True Love Coupons

Because you are so sexy, I will act out your favorite fantasy with you

special notes:

True Love Coupons

This coupon entitles you to dinner at a restaurant we've never visited before

special notes:
_____

_____

_____

_____

_____

_____

Because you inspire me, I will read you poetry

special notes:

True Love Coupons

To celebrate the summer, let's rent a boat and spend a day out on a lake

special notes:
_____
_____
_____
_____
_____
_____

This coupon is redeemable for a love note that expresses all the reasons why I love you so much

special notes:

This coupon is good for one night of uninhibited passion

Send us your coupon ideas!

What do you like to do with your true love? Send us your coupon ideas—if we use them in our next book or in future editions, we'll send you a free copy of the finished book! Submission of ideas implies free and clear permission to use in any and all future editions. Send your coupons to:

Sourcebooks
Attn: Coupon Ideas
P.O. Box 4410
Naperville, IL 60567-4410

Other great coupon books from Sourcebooks

Best of Friends Coupons

Dear Daddy Coupons

Dear Mommy Coupons

Friends Forever Coupons

Girlfriends Coupons

Golf Coupons

Hole-in-One Coupons

I Love You Coupons

I Love You Dad Coupons

I Love You Grandma Coupons

I Love You Grandpa Coupons

I Love You Mom Coupons

Little Miracles: Coupons for New
Moms and Dads

Love Coupons

Romance Coupons

Sisters Coupons

Soothe Your Stress Coupons

World's Greatest Dad Coupons

World's Greatest Mom Coupons

Also from Sourcebooks

Give these cute, little, uplifting notes of appreciation to family and friends for any reason (a job well-done, a thank you, a pick-me-up) or for no reason at all! Each note has a positive message and room to add personal notes.

A Job Well-Done!
Little Love Notes
Lunch Box Notes
You're a Star